新时代中国钢琴作品原创精粹

The Original Selections of Chinese Piano Works in the New Era

皮 黄 Pi-Huang

张 朝／曲　Composed by Zhang Zhao

人民音乐出版社·北京

SCHOTT

PI HUANG

图书在版编目（CIP）数据

皮黄 / 张朝曲. –– 北京：人民音乐出版社,2019.6
（新时代中国钢琴作品原创精粹）
ISBN 978-7-103-05488-8

Ⅰ．①皮… Ⅱ．①张… Ⅲ．①钢琴曲 – 中国 – 现代 –
选集 Ⅳ．①J647.41

中国版本图书馆CIP数据核字(2018)第036148号

丛书策划：赵易山
选题策划：张　洁、李黎东
责任编辑：张　洁
责任校对：袁　蓓

人民音乐出版社出版发行
（北京市东城区朝阳门内大街甲55号　邮政编码：100010）
Http://www.rymusic.com.cn
E–mail: rmyy@rymusic.com.cn
新华书店北京发行所经销
北京中科印刷有限公司印刷
635×927毫米　　8开　　2.5印张
2019 年 6 月北京第 1 版　　2019 年 6 月北京第 1 次印刷
印数：1－1,000 册　　定价：25.00元

作 者 简 介

　　张朝，中国当代最活跃的作曲家之一，德国朔特音乐出版有限公司签约作曲家，中央民族大学音乐学院教授，入选全国宣传系统"四个一批"人才，荣获"德艺双馨文艺工作者"荣誉称号。他是英国皇家音乐学院联合委员会、伦敦圣三一音乐学院及澳洲地区的钢琴考级首次选用作品的中国作曲家，曾应邀为盛中国、郎朗、李云迪、韩磊等著名音乐家作曲。

　　张朝生于云南，在滇南哀牢山区生活了十四年，浸染于当地各民族音乐之中。自幼酷爱美术、诗词和书法。5岁随母亲马静峰学习扬琴，6岁学习小提琴，7岁学习钢琴，10岁学习手风琴，11岁随父亲张难学习作曲。14岁起在滇池畔云南省文艺学校学习钢琴五年，在此期间创作了大量钢琴曲、小提琴曲、歌曲及乐队作品等。1987年以作曲、钢琴双专业本科毕业于中央民族学院艺术系，师从夏中汤、向世钟教授。1998年以优异成绩毕业于中央音乐学院作曲系研究生班，师从郭文景教授。曾任中国国家民族事务委员会"多彩中华"世界巡回演出团音乐总监，并在近十年的巡演中访问了欧洲、美洲、亚洲、非洲的数十个国家。

　　张朝追求民族化与个性化相结合的创作思想及本真自然的音乐风格。作品不仅荣获国内"金钟奖""文华奖""五个一工程"奖等奖项，而且还在美国、日本、澳大利亚的国际比赛中荣获多项大奖。澳大利亚ABC广播电台称其作品为"无与伦比的现代作品"。多部作品先后被收入《中国交响音乐博览》《中国音乐百年作品典藏》《中国钢琴独奏作品百年经典》。

　　在张朝的众多创作成果中，代表作有：弦乐四重奏《图腾》，钢琴曲《皮黄》《滇南山谣三首》《中国之梦》，钢琴协奏曲《哀牢狂想》，二胡协奏曲《太阳祭》，柳琴协奏曲《青铜乐舞》，琵琶协奏曲《天地歌》，第一扬琴协奏曲《盘古》，大型民族管弦乐组曲《七彩之和》，舞剧音乐《草原记忆》（合作），音乐剧《我的乌兰牧骑》，歌剧《芥子园》，合唱《春天来了》，大型森林舞台剧音乐《边城》，影视音乐《狙花女》《宝莲灯》《东方朔》《凤求凰》《四十九日祭》等。

About the Composer

Zhang Zhao is among the most active and prolific contemporary Chinese composers, currently signed to German music publisher Schott, as well as a professor at the school of music of MINZU University of China. As a recipient of many national awards and reputation, Zhang has been invited to create works for many well-known musicians, including Sheng Zhongguo, Lang Lang, Yundi Li and Han Lei. Zhang was also the first Chinese composer to have his works chosen by the ABRSM, Trinity College London and the national piano grading of Australia as official audition selections.

Zhang Zhao was born in Yunnan, China, and grew up in the Ailao mountainous region of southern Yunnan before the age of fourteen, during which period he received much exposure to local folk music. Since his youth he enjoyed a love for art, poetry and calligraphy. He began learning yangqin with his mother Ma Jingfeng at the age of five, violin at six, piano at seven, and accordion at ten. When he was eleven years old, he began studying composition with his father Zhang Nan. At the age of fourteen he entered the Provincial Arts School at Dianchi Lake for studying piano for five years. During this time he started composing and wrote a large number of works for piano, violin, vocal and orchestra. After he entered MINZU University of China, he studied with Prof. Xia Zhongtang and Prof. Xiang Shizhong, and graduated from the school of music with a double major in both piano and composition in 1987. In 1998, he completed his post-graduate study with Prof. Guo Wenjing in the composition department of the Central Conservatory of Music. Zhang later served as the music director for the "Vibrant China" world tour held by the State Ethnic Affairs Commission of China, and during a tour spanning almost a decade, he visited scores of countries throughout Asia, Europe, the Americas and Africa.

Zhang Zhao seeks to achieve a musical style that naturally fuses ethnic sounds with his own imagination. He has received numerous awards, including the Golden Bell Award, Wenhua Award, Five Ones Project Award, as well as many more for international competitions held in the US, Japan and Australia. His compositions have been commented as "Unparalleled Contemporary Works" by

ABC Radio Australia, and included in *The Chinese Orchestral Music Exposition*, *The Chinese Music Centennial Collection* and *The Centennial Classics of Chinese Piano Solo Works*.

His representative works include *String Quartet*: *Totem*, the piano pieces *Pi-Huang*, *Three Mountain Songs of Southern Yunnan* and *The Chinese Dream*, concertos for piano (*Ailao Rhapsody*) , erhu (*Song of the Sun*) , liuqin (*The Music and Dance of Bronze*) , pipa (*Song of Heaven and Earth*) and yangqin (*Concerto No.1 for Yangqin "Pan Gu"*) , a large-scale work for Chinese traditional orchestra *Harmony of Seven Colors*, dance music *Memories of the Grasslands*, musical *My Ulan Muqir*, opera *The Mustard Seed Garden*, choral music *Spring Has Arrived*, and musical drama *Border Town*. He has also scored for films and television, including music for *Flower Girl*, *Lotus Lantern*, *Dongfang Shuo*, *A Pair of Phoenixes*, and *Song of 49 Suns*, etc.

皮 黄

Pi - Huang

献给我的儿子张羽同

For My Son Zhang Yutong

(1995)

张 朝曲

Composed by Zhang Zhao

* 节奏自由，弹性节奏。

　Free rhythm, tempo rubato.

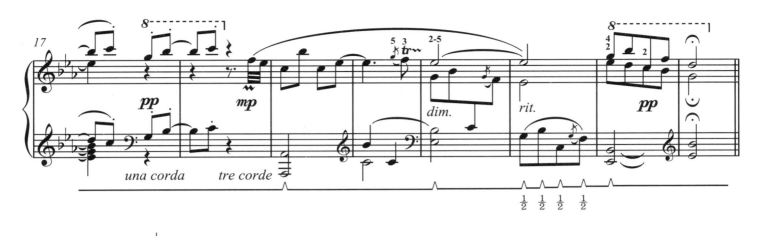

Allegro (♩ = 132) innocente

【二六】【Erliu】

Like flowing water

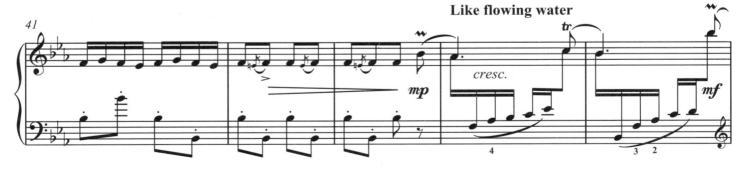

* 请合理使用踏板。
Please use pedal properly.

Allegro (♩ = 136) **zeffiroso**

【流水】【Liushui】

Spirito

【快三眼】【Kuai sanyan】

* 用拳奏。
Using fist.

4

Lento ($\quarter = 32$) a capriccio
【慢板】【Manban】

*上声部模仿钟声。
The upper voice imitates the bells.

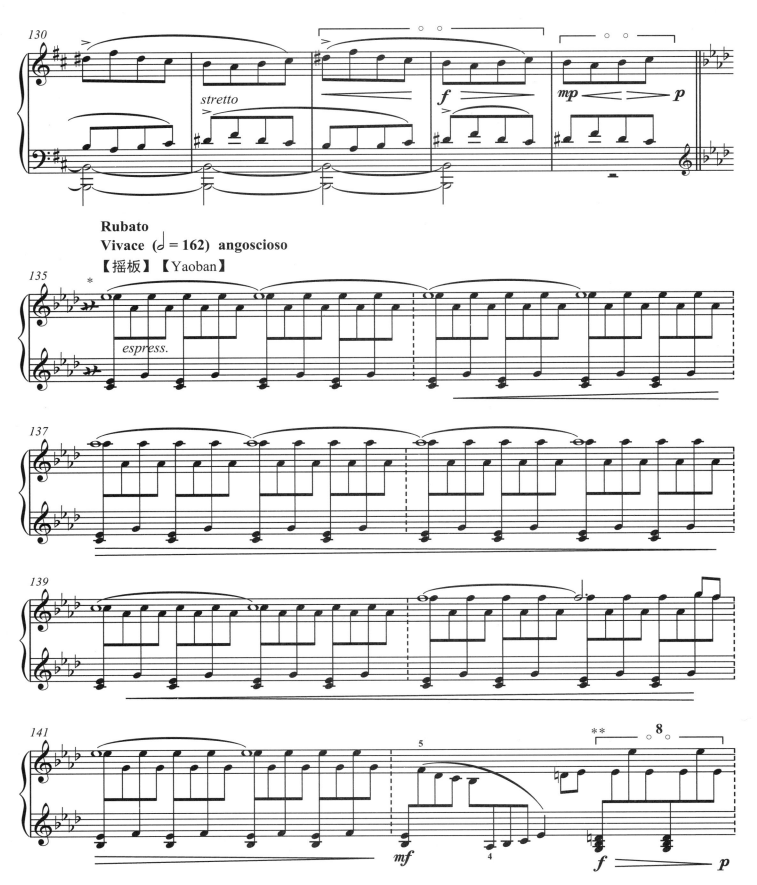

* 上声部似拖腔，内声部似京胡滑指与弹拨（即"紧拉慢唱"的效果）。可以自由延伸节拍。

The upper part is played like Tuoqiang (a Peking Opera singing style with free rhythm) and the inner part is played as Jinghu, a high-pitched fiddle, to create a particular music style, known as Jinglamanchang (fast bowing accompanies slow singing) in Peking Opera. The beat could be extended freely.

** 自由反复。中间的阿拉伯数字指反复不少于该数。

Repeat freely. The arabic number indicates the minimum number of repetitions.

10

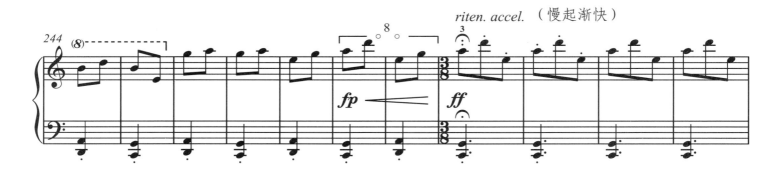

* 此处是模拟京剧脸谱中的花脸发怒时喊出的"哇呀呀……"。

It imitates the angry "wa ya ya…" voice of the role Heitou in Peking Opera.

Andante (♩ = 84) brillante

【尾声】【Coda】

Prestissimo (♩ = 138)

Allegro (♩ = 126)

* 自由反复。
Repeat freely.